AF270605

Zodiac Signs

ARIES

DiscoverRoo
An Imprint of Pop!
popbooksonline.com

by Elizabeth Andrews

popbooksonline.com/aries

abdobooks.com

Published by Pop!, a division of ABDO, PO Box 398166, Minneapolis, Minnesota 55439. Copyright © 2026 by Abdo Consulting Group, Inc. International copyrights reserved in all countries. No part of this book may be reproduced in any form without written permission from the publisher. DiscoverRoo™ is a trademark and logo of Pop!.

Printed in the United States of America, North Mankato, Minnesota.

042025
082025

Cover Photo: Splendoura Prints; Shutterstock Images
Interior Photos: Getty Images; Shutterstock Images; Wikimedia Commons
Editor: Tyler Gieseke
Series Designer: Laura Graphenteen

Library of Congress Control Number: 2024948396

Publisher's Cataloging-in-Publication Data
Names: Andrews, Elizabeth, author.
Title: Aries / by Elizabeth Andrews
Description: Minneapolis, Minnesota : Pop!, 2026 | Series: Zodiac signs | Includes online resources and index
Identifiers: ISBN 9781098247874 (lib. bdg.) | ISBN 9781098248413 (ebook)
Subjects: LCSH: Aries (Astrology)--Juvenile literature. | Ram (Astrology)--Juvenile literature. | Zodiac--Juvenile literature. | Astrology--Juvenile literature. | Astrology--Charts, diagrams, etc.--Juvenile literature.
Classification: DDC 133.52--dc23

*Scanning QR codes requires a web-enabled smart device with a QR code reader app and a camera.

TABLE OF CONTENTS

MEET THE ARIES!

Aries is the first sign of the zodiac. The yearly cycle of the sun begins here. People with the Aries sign are born between March 21 and April 19. When people ask for your "star sign," they are likely asking for your sun sign. This is the zodiac sign the sun appeared in at your birth.

Honeysuckle

ARIES

constellation
masculine
diamond
cardinal
numbers
1
9
TUES
symbol

ZODIAC CALENDAR

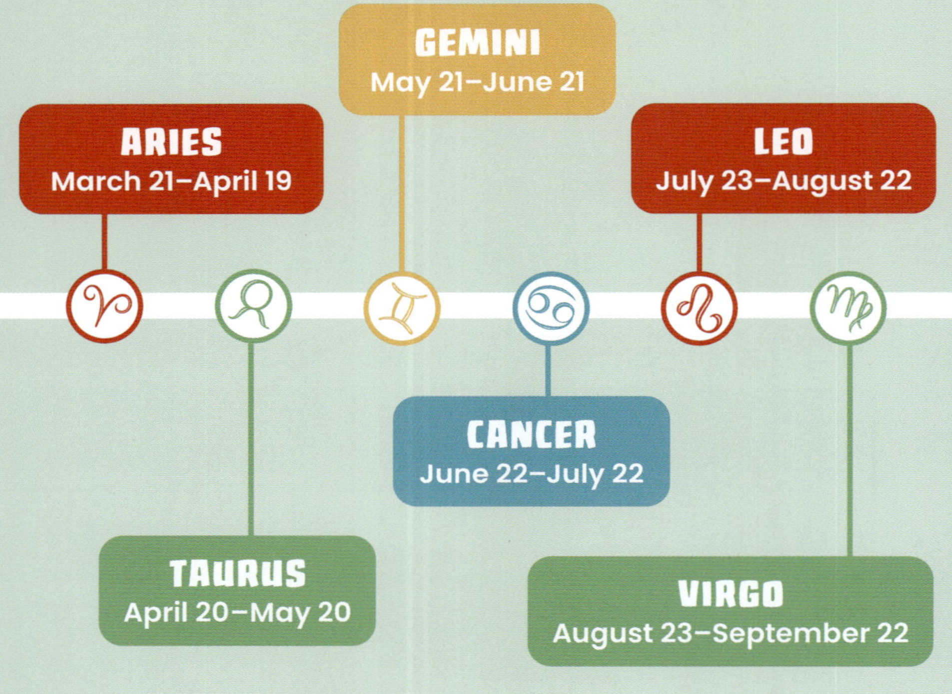

Three features help describe zodiac signs. Signs can be masculine or feminine. Each zodiac sign is given a mode. The three modes are cardinal, fixed, and mutable. Each zodiac is also

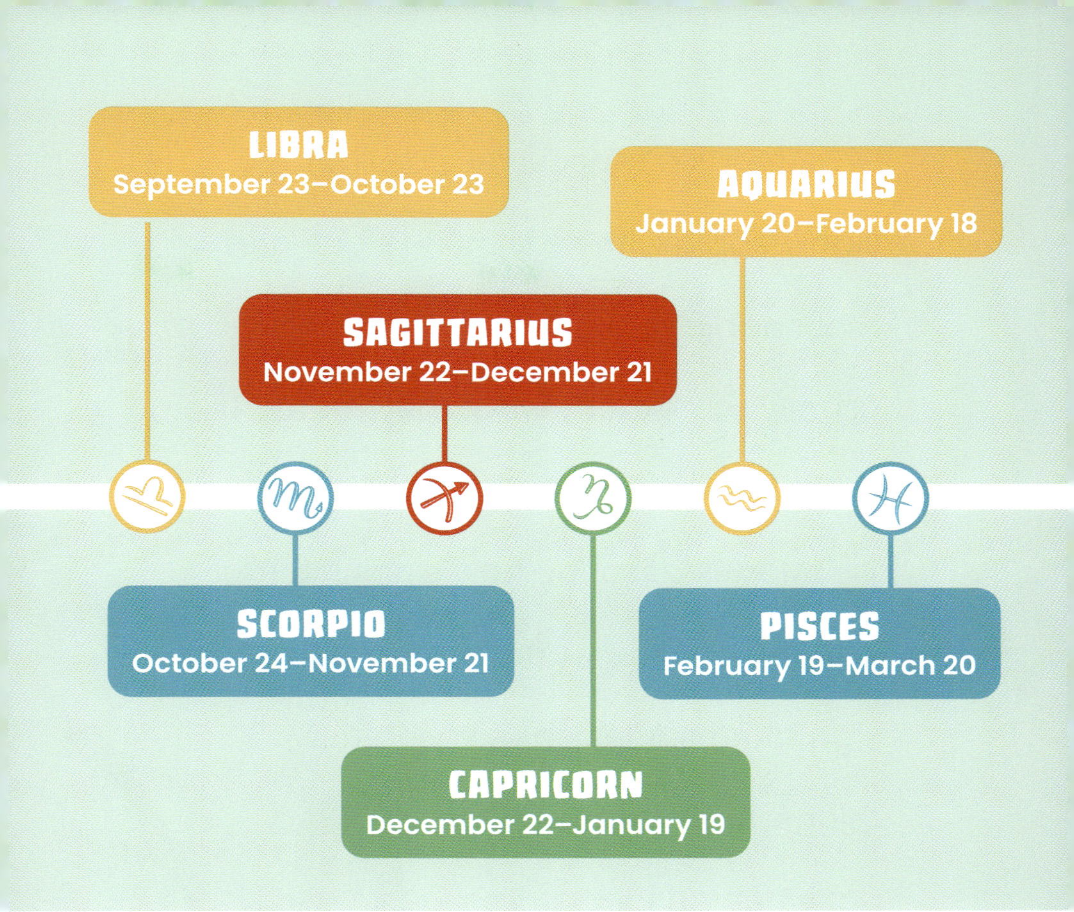

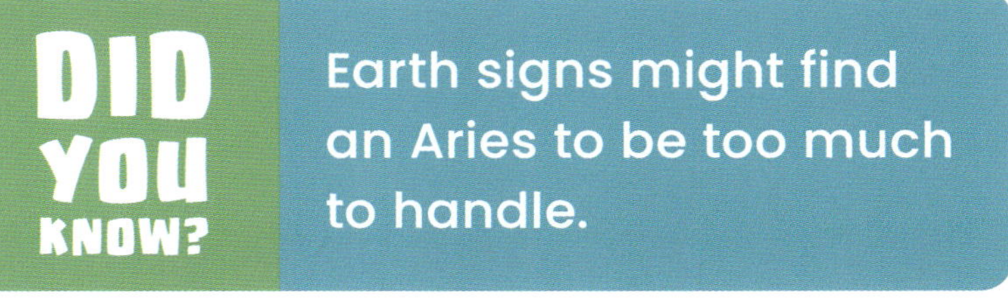

a fire, air, earth, or water sign. No zodiac
signs share the same three features.

DID YOU KNOW? Earth signs might find an Aries to be too much to handle.

Aries is a masculine, cardinal, fire sign. People with masculine signs are reasonable and action focused. They usually say exactly what they mean. They are outgoing and strong.

Modes describe how signs interact with the outside world. Having a cardinal sign means Aries enjoy trying new things. Aries are quick to act when an idea strikes. Aries are active and exciting like most fire signs. They are often bold and dramatic.

Aries have strong self-confidence. They trust their ideas will bring them good things.

Aries is **represented** by the ram.
Ancient people thought the group of stars
that makes up the Aries **constellation**
looked like a ram. Egyptians connected
the ram with their god Amon-Re. He had
the head of a ram.

Amon-Re was the king of Egyptian gods.

The Greeks believed the ram represented the golden fleece of a flying ram. Ancient **Hebrews** believed the sign represented the lamb whose blood protected their children.

HISTORY OF ASTROLOGY

Humans have searched for life's **spiritual** meaning since the beginning of time. They often looked to the stars for this. Astrology is the practice of reading the movements of planets and other **celestial** bodies and connecting them to life on Earth.

Some ancient people used the zodiac signs to predict future events.

Babylonians invented the zodiac in Mesopotamia over 5,000 years ago. Mesopotamia was the first known civilization. Babylon was one of the region's largest cities.

Ptolemy was an Egyptian man who studied the stars.

The zodiac is a belt of space around Earth that has 12 well-known **constellations**. Ancient people noticed that the sun seemed to move in front of these constellations throughout a year. The sun spends about a month in each constellation.

The constellations in the zodiac belt are Aries, Taurus, Gemini, Cancer, Leo, Virgo, Libra, Scorpius, Sagittarius, Capricornus, Aquarius, and Pisces. Together they make up the 12 zodiac signs. They are all **represented** by different **symbols**.

Islamic astrologers created new ways to map and measure stars.

THE ZODIAC WHEEL

CHAPTER 3

ADVENTUROUS ARIES

Aries is ruled by the planet Mars. This planet gives Aries courage and heart. As they are **represented** by the ram, Aries are also brave individuals who can climb to great heights. Great heights can be professional, personal, emotional, and physical successes.

Like the ram, Aries will follow hard paths to reach their goals.

Aries' most likable trait is their bravery. They love adventures. Preferably, their whole life would be an adventure.

Aries act quickly. When an exciting opportunity presents itself, they will jump at the chance and follow their hearts! Sometimes, this leads an Aries to thoughtlessness.

Aries struggle sitting still. They prefer to keep their mind and body busy.

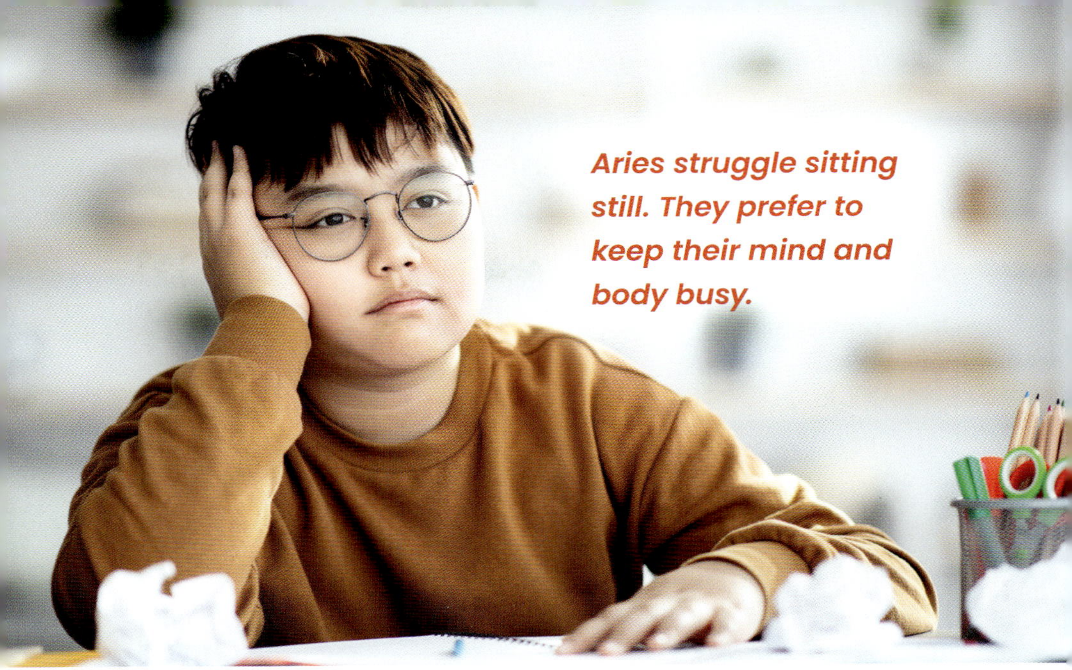

Boredom is Aries' worst enemy. They will quickly look for new adventures once boredom hits. So, Aries should surround themselves with people who bring excitement and new experiences.

DID YOU KNOW?

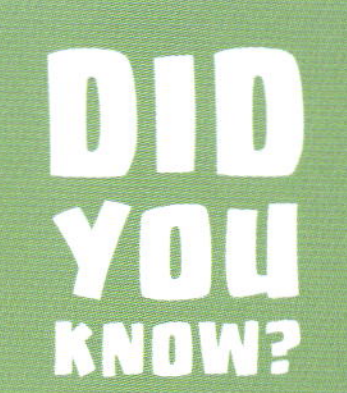

Aries will do anything if they are dared!

Aries like to be the center of attention. As fire signs, they are outgoing and talkative. They can bring excitement to any situation. Sometimes these qualities get Aries in trouble. They often speak without thinking.

Lil Nas X is a rapper and singer. He is an Aries. He shines on and off the stage in bold costumes.

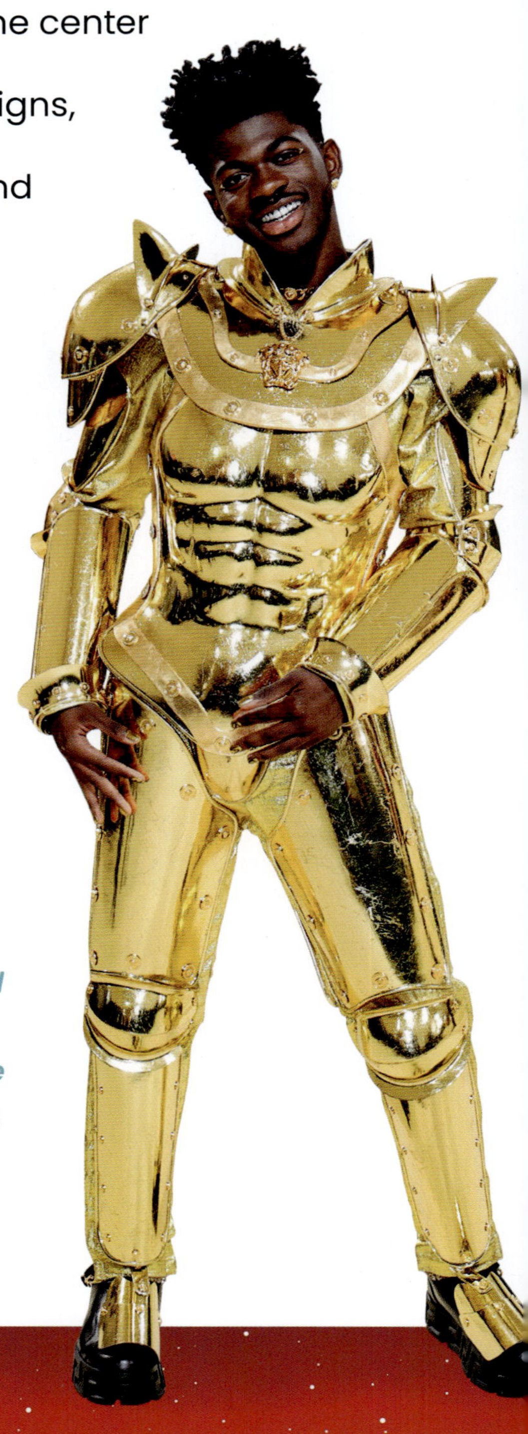

Aries love to take care of their friends. They will go out of their way to offer help when their friends need it. Aries often like to have their good deeds recognized. If there is conflict in Aries' friendships, they prefer to face the problem head on.

One of an Aries' favorite things is putting smiles on other people's faces.

BORN TO LEAD

As the first sign of the zodiac, Aries **represents** new beginnings. People with this sign might experience more forks in the road than people with other zodiac signs. An Aries might accomplish one dream or goal and then immediately be faced with another opportunity or problem.

Cardinal signs kick off new seasons. Depending on which hemisphere they are from, Aries are born in the beginning of spring or fall.

Booker T. Washington, an Aries, was born enslaved. He was freed and became a great educator and leader of his time.

Aries are natural-born leaders. Even during childhood, Aries will find chances to show off their leadership skills. They lead with their brave actions. These show other people that they can trust their Aries leaders. Aries like to work alone. They don't often share their leadership duties.

Aries tend to push themselves to succeed. It is important for an Aries to choose an exciting job that will give them leadership opportunities. They may be good firefighters, police officers, surgeons, or school principals.

As firefighters, Aries use their bravery.

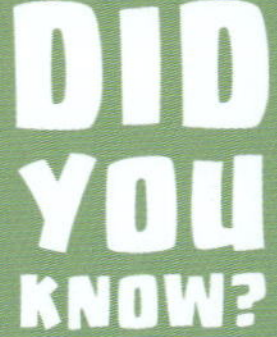

Aries are very competitive. Since they love to succeed, they will go to great lengths to make that happen. People with other signs must be careful when competing with an Aries. Sometimes, Aries get forceful to ensure success.

Aries make great athletes!

Today, astrology can answer questions about an individual. People use astrology to understand who they are and why they might do what they do. It can also help people understand others in their life. A zodiac sign can point out personal skills, possibilities, and **internal motivations**.

WHAT IS A BIRTH CHART?

Each person's birth chart contains all the planets in our solar system, the moon, and the sun. The location of where each **celestial** body was based on the exact time and location of a person's birth can be marked on a birth chart. A birth chart can explain even more about a person than what only a sun sign can. The placement of each planet affects the drive of a person. This reveals personal motivations. Astrology experts can read birth charts.

TEXT-TO-SELF

Are you an Aries? If so, do you think the sign matches your personality? If not, what do you have in common with Aries?

TEXT-TO-TEXT

Have you read any books about the other zodiac signs? How were those signs similar to and different from Aries?

TEXT-TO-WORLD

With the help of an adult, look up famous Aries. Pick one person and write a few sentences about ways that person shows Aries qualities.

GLOSSARY

celestial — having to do with the sky or outer space.

constellation — a group of stars that forms a pattern.

Hebrews — a group of ancient people living in what is now Israel and Palestine. Hebrews are related to the Jewish tribes written about in the Old Testament.

internal — of, relating to, or being on the inside.

motivation — something that makes one want to do something.

represent — to stand for or be a sign of.

spiritual — having to do with people's beliefs in things such as the soul, nature, and what happens after death.

symbol — an object or picture that represents something else.

INDEX

popbooksonline.com/aries

*Scanning QR codes requires a web-enabled smart device with a QR code reader app and a camera.